SUCCESSFULLY DEFENDING (AND WINNING) CRIMINAL AND CRIMINAL TRAFFIC CASES IN VIRGINIA

DON'T BE A VICTIM… FIGHT BACK

By O. Keith Hallam, Jr., Esq.

ISBN: 978-1-941645-51-2

Design and Published by:

Speakeasy Publications

73-03 Bell Blvd #10

Oakland Gardens, N.Y. 11364

www.SpeakeasyMarketingInc.com

888-225-8594

DISCLAIMER

This publication is intended to be informational only. No legal advice is being given, and no attorney-client relationship is intended to be created by reading this material. If you are facing legal issues, whether criminal or civil, seek professional legal counsel to get your questions answered.

NovaLegalGroup, P.C.

1507 King Street

Alexandria, VA 22314

(703) 548-1462

www.NovaLegalGroup.com

Client Testimonials

"Mr. Hallam is a superb lawyer. He did a great job for me which resulted in a good result. He is passionate about his work and clients and strives to achieve the best result. In addition to being a high caliber professional, he is compassionate and takes a personal interest in the case."

- Teji

....

"Mr. Hallam helped me out of what could have been a very bad situation for my record, future job prospects, etc. He and his office are very reliable." **- A Criminal Defense Client**

....

"Wanted to express how amazing my treatment was with Keith and his associates. He jumped on my case immediately. Got things resolved very affordably and in a timely manner without the run around I have received with prior counsel. Followed up with me after my court date which I felt was wonderful. Keith and his team are profession, prompt, and worked quickly to resolve my case. I would highly recommend Keith for your next attorney. Everything from the person receiving the calls to returning my calls was handled professionally. I would definitely choose Keith again in the future." **- Todd**

TABLE OF CONTENTS

About The Author

O. Keith Hallam, Jr. has practiced Criminal Law, Criminal Traffic Law, and Personal Injury/Accident Law for nearly 30 years – successfully representing over 10,000+ clients during this time, throughout all the courts of Northern Virginia and many other courts throughout all of Virginia. Mr. Hallam is well-known throughout this area as being one of the first, if not the first attorney, to design customized "Plans of Action" for he and his clients to pursue together, requiring that both he and his clients work as a "team," together to successfully defend and win their cases.

Mr. Hallam's customized "Plans of Actions" are designed so that both the attorney and the client have well-defined, due diligence actions and "homework" to perform, proactively, before court, so as to determine and find "holes" in the prosecution's case and for the client to engage in certain proactive actions and take certain classes before court, such as Community Service; Anger Management Classes; "Driver Improvement" Classes;

Alcohol Education Classes; and Letters of Recommendations, etc. all to place the client in the most favorable light possible when the attorney either must take the case to trial or work to negotiate a dismissal or favorable reduction of the charge with the prosecutor.

Mr. Hallam is also one of the first attorneys in Northern Virginia to put his trust and confidence in his clients, as they do in him, by designing customized "Payment Plans" to fit each client's unique financial situation.

SUCCESSFULLY DEFENDING (AND WINNING) CRIMINAL AND CRIMINAL TRAFFIC CASES IN VIRGINIA!

Don't Be A Victim..... Fight Back!!

An Overview Of Criminal Law In The State Of Virginia [Or Why Criminal Court Is Like A Casino]

Virginia Criminal Law encompasses a wide variety of offenses, including traditional categories such as theft, drugs, assault, larceny, and other charges, which are categorized as Misdemeanors and Felonies. However, in Virginia, offenses involving a motor vehicle can also be considered criminal, which most people don't realize. It's important when we discuss criminal law that we also discuss criminal traffic law.

There are Six Classes of Felonies in Virginia; Class 6 felonies are the least serious, with penalties of up to 5 years in prison; while a Class 1 felony is the most serious and can mean life in prison. These numbers may seem confusing; you might think that Class 6 felonies might be the worst and a Class 1 felony would be the least serious, but it's the other way around under Virginia law. With misdemeanors, there are four Classes; with Class 4 being the least serious, such as drunk in public; and Class 1 misdemeanors being what we typically think of as traditional "Misdemeanor charges" such as assault and battery, concealed weapon, petit larceny, trespass, etc., for which one can receive up to a year in jail and a $2,500 fine. But, what might be the most important thing to know is that when a person is charged with a minor Class 4 misdemeanor, like drunk in public, or a Class 1 felony like murder, they will all have a "Criminal Record" for the rest of their lives with the FBI, Homeland Security and all law enforcement and intelligence agencies in the United States.

There are also criminal traffic misdemeanors and criminal traffic felonies. Class 1 traffic misdemeanors, such as reckless driving, driving on a suspended license, DUI/DWI, hit and run, and eluding a police officer, can cost you up to 1 year in jail and a $2,500 fine, which is the same as other Class 1 criminal misdemeanors such as assault and battery or carrying a concealed weapon (and you will also have a permanent criminal record for the rest of your life with agencies such as the FBI and Homeland Security); as well as the possible loss of your driver's license for up to 12 months; up to 6 negative points on your DMV driving record; cancellation of your car insurance or your rates being significantly raised; which you don't face with the other aforementioned traditional "non-traffic" misdemeanors. Again these are all criminal charges resulting in a permanent criminal record, even though these types of criminal traffic cases are handled in Traffic Court in Virginia and not in criminal court.

Many people receive a Traffic Summons for many of these Class 1 criminal traffic misdemeanors, but "blow it off" as no more than a traffic ticket. They forgot, or they didn't listen, when the police officer who gave them their Summons also told them that by signing their Summons, which they must do, that they are promising to appear in court, (a mandatory court appearance), so they don't go. Therefore, several days later, they get a knock at their door and get arrested by the police on a Bench Warrant for another criminal charge; "Failure to appear" a Class 1 misdemeanor, all for what they thought was only a minor traffic infraction. This happens because all too often people don't even know that their "Traffic Charge" is really a criminal misdemeanor charge. They're shocked if they don't get a lawyer but go

to court themselves; maybe it's their first criminal traffic offense so even though they do not know it's criminal, the judge may just give them a fine and that's all. But, they still don't realize that they've also been found guilty of a criminal charge. The bad news is that they think everything is over, that all they have is a minor traffic infraction, but it isn't. It's just getting started!

Sometime later in their life, perhaps when they're filling out their next job application, or applying for a security clearance, and they check a box "No" for the question "Have you ever been convicted of any criminal offense?", not even realizing that they just "lied" on their application, because they do <u>have a Permanent Criminal Record</u> they weren't even aware of. When they were in court on what they believed was their minor traffic infraction, but was actually a criminal traffic charge of reckless driving, driving on suspended license, etc. they gave themselves a Permanent Criminal Record even though the judge may have only given them a small fine.

They won't ever get to coach their kids Little League team or a kid's football team, or help out at their school as a soccer mom or dad. Why? Because almost everywhere in the country now, you simply cannot be around other people's kids if you have a criminal record [even though you may have only paid a small fine in traffic court] When they apply to rent an apartment or house, they will also likely be rejected because the apartment management company, in most cases excludes renting to anybody with any kind of criminal record.

It's important to know that in Virginia, many things are criminal that aren't elsewhere in the country. This is probably one of the biggest issues regarding criminal law in Virginia: People get into the criminal justice System, through what they believe to be "Minor Traffic Offenses". We all speed in our cars, but can end up facing a criminal reckless driving charge or driving on a suspended license charge. Sometimes we don't pay a traffic ticket on time then our license gets suspended; and we don't even know it because we did not get a letter from the DMV informing us of our license suspension, Then later, we get pulled

over by the police because our taillight is out, or for some other minor reason and the officer sees that our privilege to drive is suspended and we face up to 1 year in jail. These are criminal things that affect people's lives daily, particularly in Northern Virginia, not carrying a concealed gun without a license or shoplifting or selling drugs. That's why it's important to understand this aspect of Virginia law - that many actions in Virginia are criminal; both in and out of a motor vehicle, more so than in most any other part of the United States. Another thing to understand about criminal law in Virginia is that the courthouse, where your case is being prosecuted, is really not a "courthouse"; it's a "casino". That's right, a casino! People must change their way of thinking, and develop a "Zen" approach to criminal law and criminal traffic law in Virginia. Everyday, the job of a criminal defense lawyer is to make 2 plus 2 equal anything but 4; i.e. since most people are very likely legally "Guilty" of what they are charged with [2 plus 2 = 4]; our job is to make the criminal charge against them go away/be dismissed; have our client found not guilty at trial; have the charge reduced to a lesser charge; or, at a minimum, work out a Plea Agreement that can keep our client from going to jail and not having a criminal conviction record.

A Virginia courthouse is like a Casino, because a Casino has an owner and the owner of a courthouse is the Government of the Commonwealth of Virginia. The Chief Judge of the Circuit Court is like the General Manager of a Casino. The court judges are like the "Pit bosses" in a Casino. The prosecutors [known as "Commonwealth Attorneys" in Virginia] are like the table dealers and croupiers at the gaming tables in a Casino; and the criminal and criminal traffic laws of Virginia are the same as the "House Rules" of a Casino - the Rules of court are tilted against you just like the odds in a Casino. To succeed in your case, you need a professional, experienced and educated "Gambler" on your side i.e.; an experienced successful and clever Attorney who knows all the "House Rules" i.e.; the laws of Virginia; knows the courthouse procedures; knows and understand the "Pit Bosses" and "Dealers", someone who knows how to help "Tilt" the odds against you in your favor; all through their knowledge and due diligence and experienced as successful criminal defense lawyer can do.

It is important in order to have the best outcome in court just as it is in a Casino, to have a customized "Plan of Action" to tilt these odds in your favor - and then beat the odds against you in the courthouse "Casino".

At my law firm, NovaLegalGroup, P.C., we have nearly 30 years of criminal defense experience; including successfully handling thousands of cases; both criminal and criminal traffic cases. We know the range of odds you face in your case, at your specific courthouse Casino. While no one can ever predict

the exact outcome of any case, and no professional attorney can say anything with 100 per cent certainty in the practice of law, with our experience we can give you a range of likely outcomes in your case and, more importantly, design a customized "Plan of Action" to tilt the odds that are naturally against you in the Casino courthouse and to tilt the odds into your favor. So, even if a client was indeed Driving while Intoxicated with a Blood Alcohol Concentration of 0.08 per cent, or more, or they obviously knew they had marijuana in their pocket; or consciously shoplifted some jewelry from a store; with our extensive experience and knowledge of how to read police reports, interpret video dash-cam; understand radar or lidar in reckless driving or DWI, breathalyzer test results; or how to interrogate witnesses; and how to interpret and utilize the law then we can to design a customized defense "Plan of Action" for our clients. But, we've also learned through the successful handling of thousands of criminal and criminal traffic cases, that we are the most successful when we also involve our clients in creating our "Plan of Action". Rather than just sitting idly by, being scared and feeling sorry for themselves, we strongly suggest that our clients that they work with us in crafting and implementing this "Plan of Action"; by having them be as aggressively proactive and diligent as we are in defending their own rights.

We tell them "Don't Be a Victim! ... Fight Back!" This allows us to tell our clients - help us to help you win your case.

For example, if someone is facing a DWI charge, we'll ask them to seriously consider doing alcohol education classes before court. We will also strongly suggest that they attend an 8-hour Virginia Driver Improvement Class and a 4-hour Reckless Driving Class and, perhaps, perform 25 hours of community service - in essence, to be proactive and do whatever it takes to get their case dismissed or reduced.

For domestic abuse cases, we'll ask our clients to take an Anger Management class. If they had alcohol on their breath when the police arrived at the scene of the domestic violence, [which is common in such cases], we'll ask our clients to also take an alcohol education class; and, if the person they are accused of abusing is willing to forgive them, then we ask that they both engage in "Couples' Counseling".

With a drug charge, we'll ask our clients to attend Drug Education classes and possibly take urine tests to show the court that they have stopped using illegal substances; and we will suggest strongly that they engage in community service to show the court that they know they have offended the people of the Commonwealth of Virginia that are prosecuting them. Why? Because they have wasted the taxpayers' money and time having to prosecute them.

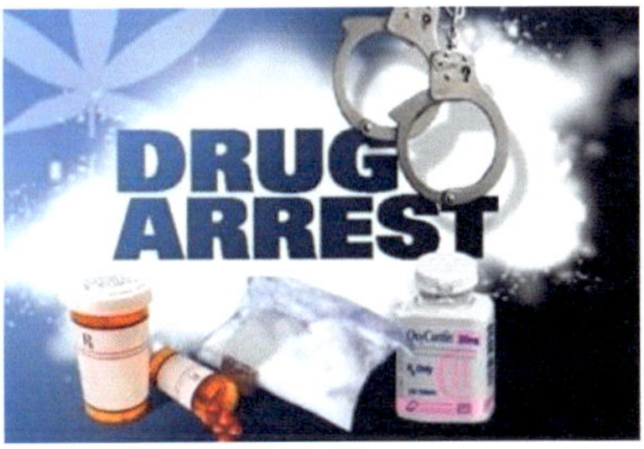

Doing this "Homework," in tandem with our due diligence of reviewing police reports, interviewing witnesses, reviewing test results, etc., is how we <u>"tilt the odds"</u> back to the client's favor.

THE MOST COMMON CRIMES WE REPRESENT PEOPLE FOR

The most common offenses that people hire us to defend them for include; DWI, Reckless Driving, and Driving On a Suspended License, on the criminal traffic side; and theft charges [petty and grand larceny], and embezzlement, drug charges ranging from Possession of Marijuana and Cocaine to possessing with the Intent to Distribute and Distribution of these and other controlled substances; assault and Battery and Domestic Assault charges; Gun charges; Credit Card Theft and Fraud charges and Bad check charges. These criminal charges represent a significant percentage of the criminal and criminal traffic charges that myself and my office have successfully handled for nearly 30 years - but, we have handled virtually every type of criminal charge that there is in Virginia - from Drunk In Public (a class 4 misdemeanor) to murder charges [a Class 1 Felony].

Are There Any Common Crimes People Are Unaware Of?

Most people do not realize that many traffic offenses, such as Driving Without a Valid License, or Driving on a

Suspended License, Hit and Run, Passing a Stopped School Bus, Eluding a police officer and, most stunningly, Reckless Driving by Speed of 20 miles per hour or more over the posted speed limit, are all serious Class 1, 2, 3 or 4 Misdemeanors.

Also, there are many other City and County Ordinances, for such actions as Possessing an Open Container of Alcohol outside at a barbecue, or Urinating in Public, that people don't realize are serious criminal offenses. People also think

that they can be outside and have had a few beers, talk loud, look disheveled, stagger a bit and that is not really a problem - and certainly not a crime But, the police do <u>not</u> need a breath or blood test to charge someone who looks and acts like that. What the police can do is charge them with Drunk In Public, which is a Class 4 criminal Misdemeanor. You don't have to have a breath or blood alcohol test showing a 0.08 per Cent BAC, or higher, like a DWI charge - all the police have to prove to have you found guilty of Drunk In Public, is that you <u>appeared to be intoxicated in a place</u> where you could be <u>seen</u> by people in <u>the public</u>. Therefore, most people are very surprised that they can be convicted of a criminal alcohol offense, like Drunk In Public without ever having had to take a breath or blood test showing their level of alcohol in their bloodstream.

Is A Person Obligated to Disclose Their Criminal Charge And Criminal Arrest Record If They Were Never Convicted?

It depends almost entirely on who is asking, and why. For instance, Government workers and contractors often have important and sensitive jobs requiring Security Clearances which, in turn, require them to self-report any criminal traffic or traditional criminal charges. On certain applications, such as business

licenses or apartment rental applications, it depends on exactly what is asked on the application. If the question is, "Have you ever been charged, arrested or convicted of any criminal offense?", or, "Have you been arrested for any criminal offense?", then you have to answer "Yes" if any of these actions apply to you, but, if the entity for which you are applying does not ask you any of these questions, then you have no duty to disclose or volunteer the information of a criminal charge. Remember, you always have to tell the truth, but you do not have to tell everything that is true, but if you must answer a question, or choose to voluntarily, then you always need to tell the truth.

How "Public" Will My Situation Be If I Am Charged With A Crime?

In Virginia, whenever a person is charged or arrested for any criminal offense, from Drunk In Public or Reckless Driving, to a DUI or Robbery, this information will be in court records and police files; and the criminal charge or arrest information is available on "Websites" and on police software programs available to anyone who knows how to obtain this information. So, the whole world can know of a charge or arrest record that is pending or any criminal conviction. Technically, anyone can find just about anything and everything about a person's criminal charge, arrest or conviction record, now pending, or in the past in Virginia; but, the good news is most people don't do that. It's not like their charge, arrest or conviction is posted on a roadside Billboard advertising that they've been arrested, charged or convicted of a crime. But, that said, the criminal information about a person is always available; and anyone motivated enough to search for that information can find it on the internet , whether it's a prospective employer, security agency, apartment rental

company, your kids' schools, your neighbors, or even your family. Of course, people talk too much. They tell their friends and neighbors, or their employers or colleagues that they got charged or arrested for something. These things can cause somebody that's just been charged and arrested, but not even convicted, to lose their job, their security clearance and their friends; as many people often want to stay away from people that have been charged, arrested or convicted of a crime. So, why advertise the fact yourself? Do as you have seen in the movies and TV. Assume there is an attorney sitting on your shoulder and whispering in your ear, two words, "Don't Talk"!

Then, there are those people, especially young people, who post their stupid and bad deeds on Facebook, twitter, Instagram and other social media. In reality, most of the time, if a friend, neighbor, colleague or boss finds out that you've been charged or arrested for a crime, it's because you made the information available, not the criminal justice system. Now you know why, in most every movie and TV show involving crimes, lawyers always tell their clients to speak to no one, except their lawyer, about their criminal charge. Sometimes, TV and movies do get it right!

Common Misconceptions About Criminal Charges

There are many misconceptions about criminal law, one of which is the role that Public Defenders play. A person qualifies for a public defender or court appointed counsel by being financially unable to retain a private attorney [read, below the poverty line], then that is the attorney they obviously must have for their criminal charge. Although Public Defenders mean well and pass the same Bar Exam, unfortunately they are almost always overworked and underpaid - and simply don't have the time or resources to dig deeply into any one particular case and use the same standard of due diligence that a privately retained attorney [such as myself and my law firm, NovaLegalGroup, P.C.] do. Since we truly get to know our clients and their cases very well; understand the law; and then create a customized "Plan of Action" for each of our clients; we believe this gives our clients the edge.

Other misconceptions come with not knowing which crimes are jailable offenses [such as not knowing that you face one year in jail for Reckless Driving, or 30 days in jail for Possession of Marijuana]; or in thinking that when you just pay a fine that you don't have a criminal record. Most people don't seem to understand what a criminal record is. Almost all of our moms and dads, when we were growing up, always told us to not get into trouble or we might get a "Permanent Criminal Record", but, sorry to tell you, mom and dad simply didn't exactly know what a Permanent Criminal Record meant. But, even though they didn't know what a Permanent Criminal Record was, mom and dad were right. If a person is ever charged, arrested and/or convicted of any criminal offense, they will indeed have an official, nationwide Permanent Criminal Record forever. In most cases, the charge and arrest can never be deleted or expunged. In Virginia, if you ever plead guilty, plead no contest, or are found guilty of any crime, their conviction record can never be expunged. If you are fortunate enough to have a really good attorney and their

case is dismissed without them having to do any terms and conditions pursuant to a judge's direction to get their charge dismissed, then they may be eligible to have the charge and arrest record expunged and deleted from their Permanent Criminal Record.

So, what is a Permanent Criminal Record? "Where is your Permanent Criminal Record kept? Who keeps it? etc. Your Permanent Criminal Record is stored with the "National Crime Information Center" [NCIC]. The NCIC is the FBI, Homeland Security, Immigration and CIA database. The NCIC is maintained forever and includes all criminal convictions, nationwide, including Virginia. As noted, it is only possible to expunge or delete a criminal charge or arrest [but never a conviction] in Virginia if your original criminal charge was dismissed with no terms and conditions attached to the dismissal.

The process for an "Expungement" involves filing a "Petition For Expungement" with the local Circuit Court where you live. There are a significant number of steps that you must negotiate through to be able to obtain an -

Expungement, and this process includes not only many difficult steps but also includes a significant amount of time. It usually takes approximately 4-6 months for the process of a "Petition For Expungement" to be concluded. But, the time, the patience and the cost involved is well worth it so that you have absolutely no permanent criminal Record whatsoever.

HOW DO CRIMINAL RECORDS FOR LOW-LEVEL OFFENSES AFFECT PEOPLE?

People can be affected in a thousand different ways by a charge, arrest or a conviction record, particularly in the Northern Virginia area, because virtually everyone in Northern Virginia is connected, in one way or another, with the Federal, State or local governments; or as a government contractor with a private company providing goods or services to the Federal, State or Local governments; or are employed in civilian jobs that require employees to not have any criminal record history at all. If you get a criminal record in Virginia, it's permanently recorded and kept in the NCIC database forever, as noted above. Those with <u>any</u> criminal record will usually not pass or get the security clearances needed for government or government contracting jobs; and they may lose any security clearance they have. Whether the person may have a "Public Trust" , a "Secret", "Top Secret", or "TS/SCI Clearance", they're likely be downgraded in clearance or lose their security clearance entirely, which will make them unmarketable in the employment arena.

One gentleman I know [not a client of mine] received a Reckless Driving Summons in Virginia some time ago; but as with most people, he had no clue that this speeding Reckless Driving was actually a criminal offense. It was his first Reckless Driving and, in fact, he had no bad driving record whatsoever. So, in all naiveté, he went to court [which is mandatory for virtually all criminal charges, though he did not know this], plead guilty to the Reckless Driving charge, and only received a $100 fine [though he was facing up to one year in jail, up to a $2,500 fine, or both, and loss of his driver's license for 6 months]. A few months later, he filled out an application to be a volunteer baseball coach at his son's 6th grade after school baseball team; only to have the Principal of the school call him two weeks later to ask him if he knew he had a criminal record. Of course, he said he didn't. However, the principal told him he definitely did - that he had pled guilty to a reckless driving in a Virginia Court some months before. The Principal went on to inform him that a Reckless Driving charge in Virginia was a Class 1 Misdemeanor [the most serious misdemeanor in Virginia] and his conviction meant that

he could not be around children at school, in any organized or volunteer capacity. The Principal said he could come to the school for "Parents' Night" and PTA meetings, but he could not coach any teams or be a "Team Parent" or even help out at any Science Fairs or Field Days, or in any way be associated with the children for school activities.

Any criminal history: criminal charge; a criminal arrest; and especially a criminal conviction, can and will affect people on many different levels of their life. Teachers will likely lose their jobs, Federal, State, City or County workers will lose their jobs. Non-U.S. citizens can be deported depending upon the nature and class of the criminal charge, etc. Since September 11, 2001, it's a different world. Before then, most applications for just about anything only asked if you had a conviction For a Felony or for any "Crime of Moral Turpitude" [meaning a lying, cheating or stealing charge]. But now, since 9/11, virtually every application for everything [jobs, security clearances, apartment rentals, volunteering to work with children], etc., not only asks about these above-noted type of convictions, but also asks, "Have you ever been charged with, arrested for, or convicted of any criminal charge!"

What Mistakes Do People Make That Hurt Their Case?

The number one mistake that people make who are charged with any criminal matter is that they simply talk too much. In America, we are raised to be courteous and pleasant, to assume and be taught that the police are "our friends"; so we tend to be open, talkative and explanatory when we talk to other people, including the police. We are, by nature, sociable and want to be helpful. However, the worst thing that a person can ever do if they come in contact with the police, in any potentially negative situation or, indeed in almost any situation, is to talk! The police ask you seemingly "harmless" and "innocuous" questions - but everything they say is an "interrogation". In essence, you are being interrogated when you talk with the police and you probably don't even know it. They listen very carefully to everything you say; they look at your body language and they are always interpreting what you say and what you do against you.

Are There Any Other Common Mistakes That People Make?

While America is clearly the greatest, the freest and the most noble country ever, it is also, at the same time, just about the only "civilized" country in the world that allows the police to routinely, and as part of their job, to lie and cheat. What? You don't believe it? Then just watch your favorite "Cops, Robbers and Lawyers" TV shows or movies. What do you think "Undercover" cops do? They assume fictitious identities; make untrue statements; and do many acts that are illegal for the common person to make, - all in the name of the law. So, the next time you get pulled over for a burned out taillight on your car; or pulled over for a red light violation remember that when the police officer approaches your vehicle, he or she are thinking that they might have stopped a drug dealer, a DWI offender, or someone driving a stolen vehicle. When the officer asks you "Where are you coming from/where are you going to, etc.?" they're not just engaging in idle chatter. They want to see what you say and how you react-

to see if you have anything to hide or have done something wrong.

These days, many people think they can talk about anything and everything that has happened to them; look at Facebook or watch any reality TV show. And often, the same people wear these "bad acts" and stupid things they have done as some kind of reverse "Badge of Honor" on their sleeves. As a society, we use to keep the things we did wrong to ourselves. We were private and individual. Now, almost everybody puts everything on Facebook and then, emails it or posts it online, for the whole world to see. Please understand that everything you say and do, everything you post on Facebook and Instagram every twitter and email that you send, can and will be used against you. The police routinely review people's Facebook pages, get search warrants for their cell phones, and check them out on Instagram, Twitter etc. if they suspect any criminal activity on their part. If you come in contact with the police, please do <u>not</u> think they are stupid. In fact, they're extremely smart and thorough. They run your name through numerous databases [the NCIC, DMV, etc.]; they

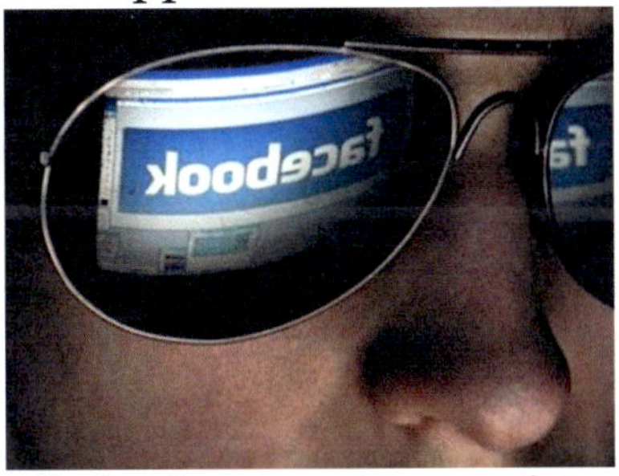

check Facebook, Twitter, Instagram and other social media. They can easily obtain all of your cell phone records. Please remember, social media is <u>not</u> your best friend - it is your worst enemy!

Another mistake many people make is thinking that they're smarter than the police. Northern Virginia is a highly educated area of the country - with some of the most wealthy and affluent counties and cities in the country. The educational level in Northern Virginia is college plus, as many individuals here have professional degrees, graduate degrees etc. So, many people in this area think to themselves that since they are obviously well-educated and successful in their professions and jobs, that they can handle anything and everything that comes their way in life - that they can handle their own DWI charge themselves; their Reckless Driving charge; their Petty Larceny charge - in fact, almost every criminal charge themselves, But Shakespeare said it better than I, or anybody, can. In one of his plays Shakespeare wrote "He who represents themselves has a FOOL for a client and an ASS for an attorney". And, that's all that people need to

know. Remember, if you're so smart, then why are you facing a criminal charge? So, don't talk to the police - get a good criminal defense attorney as soon as possible, and follow their advice. Let them do your talking for you!

The below are probably the three biggest mistakes most people make: Talking too much; posting their bad deeds on social media; and, thinking that they're smarter than the police, the prosecutor and the judge - that they can handle their criminal charge themselves. Don't be stupid...get an experienced criminal defense attorney to represent you.

How Do People Generally Discover If They Are Being Charged With A Crime?

Well, frankly, most people know they're being charged with a crime when they directly receive a "Summons" from the police in their motor vehicle or otherwise, or receive a "Warrant of Arrest" from the police or a Magistrate at the police station. Otherwise, people are contacted by the police in one of several ways. Often a police officer may come to their door, looking for them; but they think they haven't done anything wrong that they're aware of; or the police may be investigating a recent motor vehicle crime such as "Hit and Run" and want to look at a person's car and ask some questions. Then, that's the time to not talk_but to call a lawyer. When a police officer says to you, "May I search your car?" on a routine traffic stop and you hesitate and say, "Why?", the officer will answer your question with another question, saying "Well, why not? Do you have something to hide?" So, what should you do? Well, first, you should never have spoken with the officer at all. All you should have done is properly identify yourself, and provide them with your driver's license or other required

documentation. Nothing else! This is America! In America all you have to do when you come in contact with the police is simply to identify yourself properly. Nothing else! You have no obligation to talk with the police or answer any questions. If you don't talk, it's very hard to get yourself into trouble. If you do talk, you will likely make more problems for yourself.

Regarding white-collar or money crimes; or for gun or drug crimes; or large scale operations involving multi-jurisdictional law enforcement "Task Forces", by the time you find out you're under investigation, it may be too late. Indictments may have been issued by a Grand Jury, or Search or arrest warrants issued against you. People may not even

know that they're under investigation, perhaps for years. Everyone else will know because a letter comes in the mail from the local police department asking you to "stop by" the police station to just "Sign some papers". Even someone stopped by the police is not necessarily cited or arrested at the time. They may end up being investigated for something and eventually charged and arrested for a crime. So, again, don't talk!

CAN PEOPLE DEPEND ON THE "MERCY OF THE COURT" IN A CRIMINAL CASE?

The idea of throwing oneself on the "Mercy of the Court" is just a cliché; there is no substance to it whatsoever! People who say, "I'm going to throw myself on the mercy of the court", don't even know what it means. They say it because it makes them feel good; it sounds good and they try to comfort themselves because they're scared of losing their job or security clearance; or being kicked out of school, if they are found guilty of a criminal or criminal traffic charge. But the idea of "Mercy" has nothing to do with guilt or innocence. "Mercy of the Court" may come into play at the "sentencing" of the individuals, but, by then, it's too late; they have already either found guilty or have admitted the guilt and already have a criminal conviction. What they are then doing at "Sentencing" is trying to mitigate, or lessen, the criminal penalty. But, by then, they already have a criminal charge, arrest, and conviction record with the FBI and Homeland Security. To get real "Mercy" from the court, at sentencing, you have to be proactive, even

showing true remorse, if necessary, before court; not after you're found guilty and being sentenced.

At my Law Firm, NovaLegalGroup, P.C., if we win a case at trial, fantastic! But, more often, we also "Win" cases by negotiating them away so that our clients don't have a criminal conviction record. But when that's not possible, then we work with our clients to try to mitigate the penalties a client is facing at Sentencing; and that's where being a good person and doing proactive "Homework" can really come into play to reduce the sentence and lessen the chances of going to jail, or, working out a "Deferred Judgment" alternative to a conviction and jail.

Do Police Or Prosecutors Ever "Overcharge" People?

It depends on the jurisdiction, the person's actions, and their prior criminal record, if any; but yes, sometimes. In fact, in some jurisdictions, they do the opposite. They "Undercharge" a person. If somebody is caught with marijuana, of course they'll be charged with possession of marijuana; and it could be just that straightforward. But then, if the person tries to flee, or argues with the police, or refuses to identify themselves, then they may be charged with "Resisting Arrest" or "Assault on a Police Officer", or Failure To ID themselves properly, or other possible charges, Thus multiple charges can definitely stem from one event.

If you're stopped for Reckless Driving for traveling 20 miles per hour or more over the speed limit, then you'll probably be charged with Reckless Driving [a Class 1 Criminal Misdemeanor as well] But, if you're rude, abrupt, hesitate to identify yourself or refuse to give up your license to the police officer, then the officer might look to see if your vehicle registration and inspection are in order;

or they may look to find defective equipment somewhere; on your car; or look for other problems in which you may have technically violated the law - then charge you with several things. Most people are charged relatively correctly; but in many cases,

particularly drug or theft cases, officers will either Undercharge" or "Overcharge" officers for various reasons.

For example when a person commits embezzlement, they usually embezzle money from their employer a little bit at a time, often over a period of time. As a result, they could be charged with a separate embezzlement charge for each time they took money. But often, they're just charged with only one charge of misdemeanor count of Felony Embezzlement; (depending upon the amount taken each time), and thus they are "Undercharged". In some jurisdictions, the police and prosecutors believe in "Undercharging" an individual gaining them leverage to tell that person and their lawyer; that if they don't plead guilty to one charge of embezzlement, they will charge them with other numerous separate embezzlement thefts they committed individually, over time. This is done of course to take advantage of the leverage they have to "Box" a client up in to pleading guilty to the one charge.

Conversely, other jurisdictions will "Overcharge" on that same set of facts. In these jurisdictions, police and prosecutors will charge separately for each and every single individual

embezzlement transaction over time; and then say they will agree to dismiss the other charges if the person pleads guilty to one or two of the numerous charges they brought. But, in most cases, most people are correctly charged for what they do. But when police or prosecutors want to use leverage on that individual, to gain an advantage or possibly to gain additional information about their bad acts or those of others, and use pressure, then they can "Overcharge" or "Undercharge" an individual to get what they want. This is a common police and prosecutorial action in particularly serious or complicated criminal cases.

WHAT IS THE BAIL PROCESS AND HOW DOES THAT WORK?

Constitutionally, everyone is theoretically entitled to Bond; when charged with a criminal act; which is simply an old-fashioned word that means "Promise".

Virtually, everyone who is arrested will have some form of bond. In Virginia, for a fairly low or medium level crime, if the person lives in the local area, and they don't have a prior criminal record, then

likely they'll probably be released by the Magistrate on a "Personal Recognizance", "Bond" which means they'll sign a bond "agreement" with a promise to appear in court; and that if they fail to appear, not only will they be subject to the criminal charge of "Failure to Appear", but they will also have to pay the city or county where they are arrested the amount of bail "Bond" that they promised to pay if they did not appear.

But, for higher level crimes or, if the person charged has a prior criminal record, or lives out of state, then the Magistrate may not give them a "Bond"; so they will have to be held in Jail and then go in front of a judge, where the judge the next business day, where the judge decides whether or not they should be granted "Bond" and how much the "Bail" should be; and most people do qualify for some type of "Bond"

At the end of the day, Bail and Bond are determined by two basic things: a) That there is a reasonable expectation that the person charged will appear for all of their required court dates

and not flee the jurisdiction prior to trial; and, b) that there is a reasonable expectation that the person is not a threat to the community or society if they are released on Bond.

If you or your family cannot afford to put up their own Bail Bond money [which is returned to you or your family, in full, at the end of your case - as long as you do not flee], then you can obtain the services of a Bail Bondsman who will charge you or your family a non-refundable fee of usually 10 percent of the Bail amount; which they keep as their fee to guarantee that the full amount of the Bail Bond will be paid to the court if you fail to appear in Court at any Court date, or breach any other bond requirements.

"A STEP – BY – STEP ANATOMY OF THE CRIMINAL PROCESS IN VIRGINIA"

The first thing everyone should do, especially if they're stopped or contacted by the police, is to keep quiet and not talk to the police or anyone about their situation, [except maybe their "significant other" that you can absolutely trust], and an attorney. People love to talk, but and letting people know

you're now charged with a criminal offense is just about the second worst thing you could do. What is the first worst thing you could do, Talking about your criminal case on "Social Media" [Facebook, Twitter, Instagram or any other Social Media].

Of course, the second thing you want to do is hire an experienced criminal defense attorney as soon as you can. One of the best ways of finding the most experienced Criminal defense attorney for you, in your local area, is to "Google" "Criminal Defense Attorneys in (your area)" for your type of case, then call and interview several attorneys on the phone - find out if they will take your call personally - or they only want you to talk to their secretary to book you for an appointment - and will not talk about your case on the phone. Find out if they will talk to you for a while on the phone; about your case, about you, about your life, your job, your needs and wants in relation to the criminal charge you have. If they give you guidance, comfort and direction regarding your case; and, if you are comfortable with your conversation with the attorney, then make an appointment, in person, but only if they offer you a Free Consultation and a "Payment Plan" for their fee, that meets your financial needs.

As the senior attorney and owner of my own law firm, NovaLegalGroup, P.C., whenever a new potential client calls my office, myself, or one of my experienced attorneys, will always speak to you on the phone for as long as necessary to get all of details of the charge, and then begin to give you the outline of a customized "Plan of Action" to deal successfully with your case. We then explain the law to you and how we would handle your case - as well as quote you a reasonable fee and a "Personalized Payment Plan" to meet your personal and financial needs. We then, invite you to meet with us, in person, to work out the details of

your customized "Plan of Action" to get your criminal or criminal traffic charge, dismissed or reduced to a significantly lesser charge, or a lesser penalty.

For criminal misdemeanors, people will either receive a Summons, which looks much like a "Traffic Ticket" or, they will receive an Arrest Warrant. An Arrest Warrant is exactly what it sounds like;

the person has been arrested for a criminal misdemeanor or felony, and are fingerprinted and photographed and their arrest information will have been put into the FBI and Homeland Security's "National Crime Information Center" [NCIC] database, as having been charged and arrested for a crime.

As mentioned, a Summons looks like a traffic ticket and can be used not only for criminal traffic offenses such as a DUI or Reckless Driving, or for traditional Misdemeanors. However, most traditional criminal Misdemeanor charges are made by an Arrest Warrant, just like a felony, where the person is physically arrested, booked at the jail, fingerprinted and photographed; have their charge and arrest put in the NCIC; and have a Bond set by the

Magistrate. The procedure for Misdemeanors in most jurisdictions is then to have an "Arraignment' or 'Advisement" several days after the person has been formally charged. This is where the person charged appears in front of a judge, in court, or sometimes in the jail by video, who then advises them of the seriousness of the criminal charge, the maximum penalties, they face, and that they should to obtain the services of an attorney to protect their rights. If they are below the "Poverty Line" set by the Federal government and can't afford an attorney, the Court will then appoint one for then.

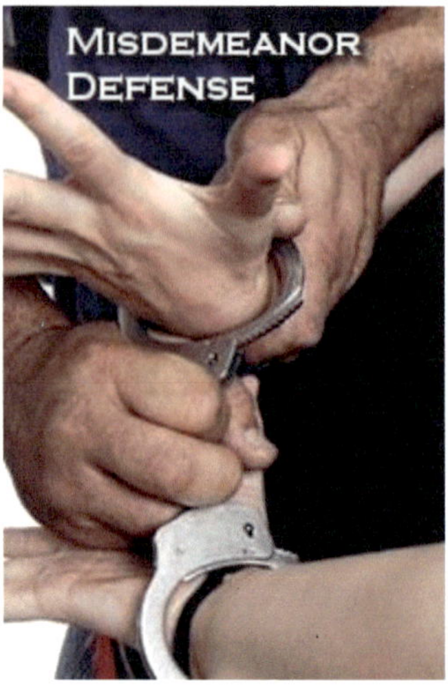

A misconception many people have is that they think if they don't have a job, or they are a college student, that they'll automatically get a Public Defender or Court-Appointed attorney, which isn't necessarily true. The Court, at the Arraignment or Advisement has them fill-out a Financial Statement to disclose all of their assets and income, and that of the people they live with or who support them; and then determine if the person is entitled to a Public Defender or Court-Appointed Counsel. For instance, if they live with their family, or with others, who contribute to their support, but they're not working or in school, then the car, home, bank savings and any income from those they live with, and who participate in some way in their support, will also be factored into their Financial Statement to determine whether or not they are really "below the "Poverty Line". After that, a trial date is set on their charge and usually held within 1-3 months from the date they were charged.

For a Felony, there will always be an Arrest Warrant issued never just as Summons; which results in the person being charged and arrested; then taken to the police station or detention center where they

will be fingerprinted and photographed, and all of their information will be entered into the NCIC/FBI-Homeland Security database. At that point, they will have some type of Bond set by the Magistrate, who works out of the jail; and, after Bond is set and bail is met, they will then attend Arraignment in front of a Judge, several days after they've been released on a Bail Bond. During the Arraignment, the judge will explain to them the seriousness of the

Felony charge, that they can go to prison, and that they need to obtain a lawyer by a specific date. They will also fill out a Financial Statement, as noted above. If they truly cannot afford a retained attorney, a Public Defender; a Court-Appointed attorney will be appointed. If they don't obtain the services of an attorney by the date set at the Arraignment by the Judge, [known as the Information on Attorney Date], then their Bond can be revoked and they can be put in jail until their next scheduled court date, known as a "Preliminary Hearing".

A Preliminary Hearing is handled in what is known as the "lower court", the General District Court. The "lower court" is where all Misdemeanors, Traffic and Criminal Traffic charges and Juvenile and Domestic Relations cases start but, this is where felonies <u>start</u> but do not necessarily end. A preliminary Hearing is also known as a "Probable Cause" hearing, because it is the judge's job to evaluate the evidence produced by the prosecutor at the Preliminary Hearing to determine if the prosecutor has set forth sufficient "Probable Cause" to believe that a felony has been committed; and that the individual charged is more likely than not the person who committed the felony. "Probable Cause" simply means that it is more likely than not that a Felony has been committed. If the Judge finds there is Probable Cause [and they almost always do], then the judge "Certifies" the person to the higher "Circuit Court" for a Grand Jury to hear evidence about the felony from the prosecutor, in private, and then to determine whether or not there is Probable Cause for the felony charge or charges to go forward to trial in the Circuit Court.

At the secret Grand Jury hearing, the prosecutor presents very limited and basic facts to the Grand Jury, usually with no participation by the person charged, or their attorney; and they virtually always find the necessary "Probable Cause" and will the issue a "True Bill of Indictment" against the person to start trial in Circuit Court. There is an old legal expression, which is very true, and that is that a good Jury would indict a "Ham Sandwich", if a "Ham Sandwich" was presented by the prosecutor to the Grand Jury for indictment. In essence, a

Grand Jury simply "Rubber stamps", whatever the prosecutor wants. When the Indictment is issued by the Grand Jury, the person charged with the Felony is given a date to appear in the Circuit Court, with their attorney; this date is known as a "Term Day", this

Term Day in front a circuit court judge is a date when the actual trial date will be selected [which could be as much as up to 6 months in the future, or more]. If you have a Plea Bargain arranged before at a trial date, or you plead guilty, plead no contest or you're found guilty by a judge, then sentencing will usually occur approximately 2 months after your court date. The judge, on the trial date, orders that a "Pre-Sentence Investigation" report [PSI] be prepared by the Probation Office. A PSI is where the probation Officer is assigned to the person's case and reviews their entire background; social, educationally, work history and any <u>prior</u> criminal record. All of this information in the PSI is taken into consideration by the Judge in fashioning a sentence at the sentencing date approximately 2 months after the trial or disposition date. The Judge is also presented by the defendant's attorney and the prosecutor with information regarding Virginia's

"Voluntary Sentencing Guidelines". The judge does not have to follow the "Guidelines" when sentencing an individual for a Felony, but they almost always do. If a Judge does decide to depart from the "Guidelines", upwardly by giving a harsher sentence then the "Guidelines" would suggest; or conversely if the Judge departs downwardly from the "Guidelines" to give a less harsh sentence than the "Guidelines" suggest then the Judge must put his or her reasons on the Court Record for making such departures from the "Guidelines".

If a person is found guilty at a trial in which a Jury is sitting, then they will be immediately sentenced by the Jury. After that the Judge orders a "Pre-Sentence Investigation Report" to be prepared and approximately 2 months later, the Judge will review the Jury's sentence and the "Pre-Sentence Investigation Report" about the individual convicted. The Judge is looking to see if the jury's decision comports with the law and the evidence presented. A Judge virtually never undoes or disturbs a Jury's sentence; rather they almost always let it stand -

because a jury is a group of one's peers and neighbors has that been legitimatized by Constitutional standards and our society.

How Long, On Average, Does A Misdemeanor Or A Felony Take To Go From Start To Finish?

Misdemeanors usually take 3-4 months from the date the person is charged, to the date of trial; while felonies virtually never take less than 6 months - and generally will take up to 12 months and sometimes more, from the date of arrest to the date of final sentencing, as noted above. It should also be noted that there are at least 6 steps to every felony if it is not plea-bargained at the Preliminary Hearing, and goes to trial or disposition and sentence in the Circuit Court.

WHAT PERCENTAGE OF CRIMINAL CASES GO TO TRIAL.

It is commonly accepted that no more than about 5 percent of all criminal cases [Misdemeanors and Felonies], ever go to trial.

The other 95 per cent of cases are either dismissed, or a plea bargain is arranged between the defendant, their attorney and the prosecutor for a final compromised disposition - which usually results in either the case

being set for a Deferred Judgment and dismissed at a future date if complied with the terms of the Deferred Judgment; or, is reduced to a lesser charge than the one that the person was charged with. The reality of this is that while I would like to tell you that almost everyone charged with a crime is “Innocent” of that crime, the reverse is unfortunately true: Very few people are really “Innocent”. Rather, they are likely guilty as charged.

Often, we use the word “Guilty” in the wrong way. “Guilty” is a word of art in the law; a finding made by a judge or jury or to which you Guilty to. Most people who are accused know that they; stole something from the store (larceny); or that they drove with a Blood Alcohol Concentration of 0.08 per cent or higher [DUI]; or that they went 20 miles, or more, over the speed limit [Reckless Driving]; or that they had marijuana in their pocket [Possession of Marijuana]? Of course, they do! What criminal defense attorneys do is work to get their client's criminal charge dismissed through their experience, investigation and due diligence, such as talking to witnesses, reviewing all police records and test results, etc. Often, a criminal defense attorney, such as myself and the attorneys in my law firm, can find "Holes" in the cases brought against our clients by the police and the prosecutor; so even though the person is actually technically, morally, and practically "Guilty" of the crime for which they are charged, the prosecution may not be able to prove all of the elements of the crime or crimes beyond a "Reasonable Doubt", and therefore, we may be able to get their charge dismissed or significantly reduced because of our due diligence and experience. Take the O.J. Simpson case, for instance; it's a perfect example of good

lawyering and the ability to have a person's charges dismissed at trial when, in reality, they were "Guilty" of the charge.

Our job, as criminal defense attorneys, does not depend on whether the person did, or didn't do, what they're charged with; but rather, whether or not the prosecution can prove every single element of every criminal charge beyond a "Reasonable Doubt"; which is required by the United States Constitutions; and often the prosecution cannot do so. If we can find just <u>one element</u> of their charge, for the crime they are charged with, which the prosecutor cannot prove beyond a Reasonable Doubt, then we'll get the charge dismissed! We may find something that the police or prosecutor did incorrectly, or forgot to do; or perhaps paperwork that wasn't done properly or was not done at all, or, there is a lack of complete evidence or good witnesses in the case; or perhaps there were incorrect or disputed test results of some kind [blood tests, drug tests, forensics tests etc.]. Then, if we find any of these problems with the police or the prosecution's work, in favor of our client, we may have the case dismissed; or

work out a "Plea Bargain" resulting in the criminal charge eventually being *nolle prossed*/dismissed; or, a "Deferred Judgment" entered for eventual dismissal; or the charge being reduced to a lesser charge.

In addition to the legal due diligence we do, we also strongly suggest to our clients that they do a number of "Homework" assignments that will put them in the very best light possible for presentation of their case to the prosecutor and the Judge and for any potential plea

negotiations that may have to be engaged in to help our client get their charge dismissed, or reduced to a lesser charge. This "Homework" that we have our clients do is proactive actions in which they are reeducating and in essence are "punishing" themselves all before their Court date. This Homework does not cause them to admit guilt, or be held against them, in fact exactly the opposite - it puts them in a much better light with the court than if they did not do such "Homework". The "Homework" that we give them to do depends on the nature of the charge and any prior Criminal, or bad driving record, that they may have and, may involve such things as: doing Community Service in the Court jurisdiction where the charge exists is; drug or alcohol classes; anger management classes; restitution of any moneys out of pocket by the victim or the State as a result of the client's actions; driver improvement classes; counseling of some sort etc. All of this "Homework" is a huge step towards a much better disposition of the client's case than if they did not engage in such "Homework", when trail is not an option.

When you retain an experienced and successful defense attorney such as myself and my Associates at NovaLegalGroup, P.C., then it becomes a team process. In my Law Firm, we truly work as a "Team" with our client.

It is interesting to note that when you consider the manpower, time, money and effort it would take for every case in the judicial system to go to trial, the judicial system would simply break down and grind to a halt. There aren't enough judges, courtrooms, prosecutors, police and investigators available to handle every case if it went to trial. Therefore, there are a lot of incentives for the Commonwealth of Virginia to be moved towards a position where they

actually want to work out a final disposition with the criminal defense attorney, for their client, to get their charge reduced, dismissed or worked out prior the trial disposition date, Otherwise, the court system would be working 24 hours a day, weekends and holidays. Also, the state budget simply isn't there to do this for the Commonwealth of Virginia or any State, or even the Federal Government. So, the prosecution has limited time and resources to devote to the handling of the tens of thousands of cases that they have every year; and the hundreds or even a thousand or more cases any one prosecutor may have each year in the Courts of Northern Virginia.

CRIMINAL LAW

So, the criminal justice system, in an attempt to manage the massive volume of cases it has, does have many incentives to consider dismissing or reducing criminal charges if they are prepared and presented in the most efficient, best and complete way by a criminal defense attorney. This is one of the reasons why many charges are dismissed or worked out when they're presented properly by an experienced legal team.

WILL A PRIOR MINOR CHARGE AGGRAVATE A CURRENT CRIMINAL CHARGE?

Virginia is considered by most attorneys to be one of the toughest states in the country when it comes to criminal and criminal a traffic law; so the answer to this question is, yes! To a defense attorney, it seems like almost everything that a person can do in Virginia is "Criminal" in nature. While this is an overblown statement, it is more the case here in Virginia, than in most other states - that the number of things that can be engaged in Virginia, that may be criminal, and the degrees of criminality, are much more serious than other states. That's particularly true when Virginia is compared to Maryland or Washington D.C., in comparison, Virginia is brutal, tough, and almost unforgiving when it comes to the nature and scope of criminal and criminal traffic law.

Even a prior conviction for a very minor criminal charge, such as Drunk In Public, (Class 4 Misdemeanor) or possession of Marijuana, (Class U Misdemeanor), both of which are relatively low - level Misdemeanors, will be held against a person if they are subsequently charged with another crime during their lifetime.

During our first interview with prospective the client on the phone, we will ask them if they have any prior criminal record anywhere, whether in Virginia or in another state. I ask them to be completely truthful and think back throughout their life. Even if they committed a minor criminal offense many years ago, the prosecutor will find out about it through the NCIC, and will hold it against them in their current case. Even a minor Juvenile Court Conviction 20, 30 or 40 years ago, will now be held against them. When I tell a potential client this, they can't believe it. They have always heard that if a crime is committed when they're a juvenile, then their criminal record will be sealed and never used against them by anyone. This is simply not true. It is true that a person's juvenile record is not available for public view and that prospective employers, apartment rental companies, security agencies, and such cannot get access to a person's juvenile record anytime. But, a prosecutor or law enforcement officer can "pierce the veil" of juvenile court and are always able to obtain information about a person's

prior juvenile conviction to use against them in court, in Virginia.

This is usually a shock to our clients, and to almost everyone else. So, even if you're 80 years old now, and you were charged with possession of marijuana when you were 14 and found "Involved" by a Juvenile court, the prosecutor can use it against you now. They do detailed criminal background checks on everyone who has a charged criminal charge [with

the exception of criminal traffic charges, in which they only check Virginia DMV records]. For criminal traffic charges like : DWI; Reckless Driving; "Hit and Run"; etc. prosecutors will obtain a person's 11-year personal DMV Driving Record and hold anything they find on the person's 11-year driving record against them for the past 10 years. Otherwise, for every other criminal charge, prosecutors obtain a printout from the NCIC, which has everything a person has ever been convicted of in their entire life. So, even if it happened -many years ago, in Virginia the prosecutor can use it against you, the same as if you had committed the prior crime yesterday! Prosecutors will use it to decide whether to prosecute you;

and to help decide how aggressively they may choose to prosecute you; or, how many charges they might choose to bring against you, if there is more than one charge they can bring.

If you do have a prior criminal record, the prosecutor will come after you much, more aggressively than if you didn't have any criminal record at all. And, your prior criminal record is always held against you for "<u>sentencing</u>" purposes,___if you are convicted, regardless of how long ago your prior convictions were; even if you were a 13 or 14-year old in juvenile court at that time. In essence, everything you've ever done wrong or bad that has ended up in the criminal judicial system, anywhere in the country, will be is held against you the in Virginia courts.

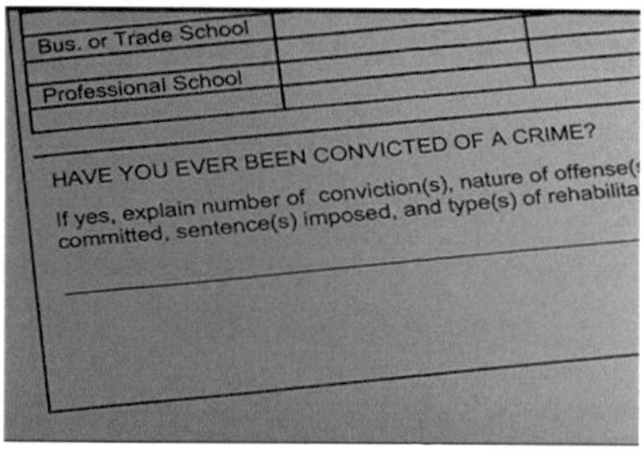

Can You Provide Some Examples of Cases Where You Prevailed Against Tough Odds?

When I first started practicing law, I was consulted by a gentleman who was charged with a DUI. It was his first offense, but he had a high Blood Alcohol Content (BAC); and his driving behavior, when he was stopped by the police officer, was, in a word "Terrible". It looked like a very tough case to "Win". I did my legal due diligence; looking at the prior breath test results for the two months before my client blew in to the alcohol breath machine at the police station - to see if I could find any anomalies, errors, service problems etc. with the breath test machine that I could use to undermine the credibility of the high blood test result against my client. But, there weren't any anomalies, errors, service problems or maintenance problems with the machine.

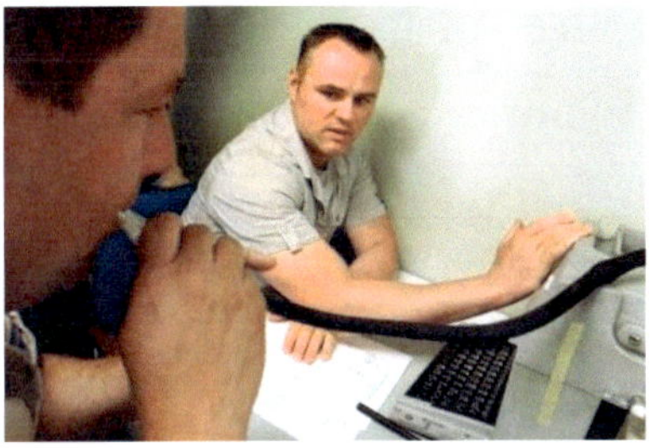

It looked like my client and myself were in a very, tough position. But I continued to look into every possible way to get the best outcome possible for my client. I looked at the police officer's "Criminal Complaint" form filed by the police officer who stopped my client; to first find out why he was stopped; in essence, to see whether or not there was “Reasonable Suspicion” for the police officer to stop my client in the first place. Again, there was bad news - the “Criminal Complaint” showed that my client had been weaving badly in and out of his lane; his headlights were not turned on; and, he was speeding. Then, I looked at how my client did on the “Field Sobriety Tests” that the police officer had him do on the roadside and the Preliminary Breath Test (PBT) results, done on the roadside; that the officer had noted. Everything I looked at was all bad. There was nothing good in the police notes, the Field Sobriety Tests, or on the Preliminary Breath Test. As I looked at all of this, it certainly did not look like a winnable case.

But, some weeks after my client was charged, and after I had engaged all the above legal due diligence prior to my client's court date, I happened to be in court, on another case, I happened to run into the same police officer who had stopped and arrested my client for the DUI case. We started talking in the hallway and he asked me to come to his office so he could show me something. When I got there, he showed me pictures of my client taken at the police station the night of the DUI arrest. My client was dressed up in a Santa Clause" costume, from an earlier Christmas party. To my amazement, the photos showed him dressed up exactly like Santa Clause, a fake white beard and all; but instead of carrying a bag of toys over his shoulder, the picture showed him handcuffed to a pipe, sitting on a bench, in the jail, "Drunk Tank". With this information, and the "Santa Clause jail" pictures, I was able to get the prosecutor to agree to reduce the criminal DUI charge down to a non-criminal, minor traffic infraction, why? Because sometimes even though a person is guilty of what they're charged with, and all of the evidence is against them, even a prosecutor will have a heart when it comes to giving "Santa Clause" a break.

Any Other Interesting Examples?

Every case is interesting in some way; one of the most interesting examples of what I consider "Good Lawyering" is a case in which a woman from California hired me, some years ago, to fight a charge of Felony "Pandering “she had, “Pandering” is the charge of being a “Pimp”. My client had been running ads in the Yellow Pages, for a number of years, advertising a very high class “Escort Service” in the Northern Virginia area.

While my client lived in California, she actually ran various “Escort Services” around the country. She would simply travel around the country Several times a year, to go to each city in which she had an “Escort service” operation, to pick up the money she had made as the “Escort Service” owner. The girls that were in her “Escort Service” were all physically beautiful girls, with no criminal record and all that had post-college degrees; which is exactly what as she had advertised. She called me from California and told me she'd been arrested and charged in the City of Alexandria with Felony “Pandering” after two of her “Girls” were caught in a police “Sting” operation, and had “Rolled Over” and named her as the “Madam” of the Escort Service - and had agreed to testify against her. After I agreed to take the case, she gave me all the details about herself and her “Escort Service” activities in the City of Alexandria.

Indeed, two of the girls had "Rolled Over" on her to save themselves from being charged with "Prostitution", as I was walking into the courtroom for her Felony Preliminary Hearing, I knew intuitively that there was something I was missing - that there was something that could help my client, that I just quite didn't see until then.

It must be noted that her "Pandering" charges simply don't happen every day. In fact, I would hazard a guess that most criminal defense attorneys have never ever in a career of 20 or 30 years have ever handled a "Pandering" charge. My legal mind said that the prosecutor had a perfect case against my client; there were two "Girls" Rolling over on her; saying that they had received all of their instructions and directions from my client; that my client had set up the "Dates" for each of them in advance with their "Johns"; and, that the Girls had to pay my client by sending half of the cash money they received from the "Johns" for their services to a specific Post Office box in a suburban Maryland Post Office. As noted before, my client would travel around the country about several times a year, picking up her earnings from various post boxes in major cities around

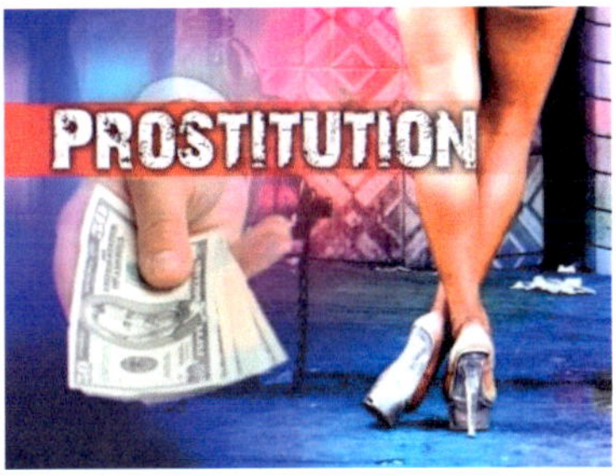

the country. So, as I was walking into the courtroom literally reading and re-reading the "Pandering" statute, one of the legal elements of the charge of Pandering hit me like a lightning bolt.

While all of the evidence and witnesses were against my client, I noted that one of the elements of "Pandering" that the prosecutor had to prove beyond a "Reasonable Doubt" was that my client had to actually receive the earnings her "Girls" prostitution in Virginia, but, my client had her "Girls" send their earnings to a Post Office box in Maryland, not Virginia; in fact, the Prosecutor, at the Preliminary Hearing, even had a federal Postal Inspector as a witness, with video that showed my client picking up the money and putting into her purse. But, the statute in Virginia for "Pandering" clearly stated that one of the elements necessary to be found guilty of "pandering" beyond a "Reasonable Doubt that the "Pimp" must receive her monetary proceeds in Virginia. My client hadn't. In fact she had, received the money in Maryland, as the prosecutor's own evidence showed by the Federal Postal Inspector's video of her picking up that money in

the Maryland suburban Post Office box. So, I pointed out these facts to the prosecutor, who had marshaled all of the facts and witness against my client; but had forgotten the part of the statute that required he prove that the money she received be received had to be received in Virginia. The prosecutor was embarrassed but obviously had to do the right thing. He immediately dismissed the cases against my client.

This was probably one of the most "Zen" dramatic moments I've had in my career. When you're looking at all of the elements of a crime. When you are completely "under the gun" and your client is about to be convicted of two major Felony Charges of "Pandering and go to prison for many years, then and to suddenly clearly see the way out was stunning.

Do People Realize the Severity of Their Criminal Charge?

People often don't realize what a criminal charge actually is, especially criminal traffic charges. They see the charge only from their point of view; but not from the point of view of the prosecutor, the police, the Judge or society; which is crucial. A large part of my job is to educate my clients; to get them to get outside of themselves and see things as everyone else sees them, not just how they see it; To see their actions and the law, but also to get rid of their defense mechanisms, excuses and fears - and then get down to the business of looking at this case from everybody else's position, which is really the one that counts. What we need to do is to get the client outside of themselves and see how the charge looks from the police point of view; the prosecutor's point of view; the Judge's point of view; and the community's point of view; then, we can then begin, in earnest, to work together as a team to get their charge dismissed or reduced.

People often simply don't see things from another person's, or society's, point of view. They don't realize that they're thinking only about themselves getting jailed; or fired from their job and/or losing their family - and they're thinking of nothing else. While these are all very legitimate concerns, they must move beyond that. Yes, they may very well get jailed or fined, or worse, since we're talking about criminal charges, but that's not the point. The point is even if they're found guilty, or plead guilty or no contest, they will have a conviction record in the National Crime Information Center, Homeland Security, FBI Database, for the rest of their lives; and this fact would be held against them when they're looking for a jobs in the future; trying to obtain a security clearance; or volunteering for coaching their kids in sports; etc. They often won't even realize why they didn't get that job in the future, or why their neighbor was not comfortable living next door to them.

One more thing: In Northern Virginia; we have huge immigrant populations, which most people don't think about. People who are <u>not</u> U.S. citizens, but who receive a criminal conviction, will likely have major immigration consequences - everything from not getting their "Green Card" or work permit renewed; to not being allowed re-entry to the United States; not getting their Citizenship, or even being deported, the U.S. Immigration and Naturalization Service does not view Felonies and Misdemeanors the way Virginia law and courts do. Some Virginia State Misdemeanors can be considered Aggravated Felonies under Immigration Law. Also, if a non-U.S. citizen is sentenced in a certain way, this can also trigger immigration consequences that can cause them to be deported or barred, which is why it is really important that non-citizens know this. It must be explained to them.

In fact, the U.S. Supreme Court ruled several years ago that criminal defense lawyers, such as myself and my firm, will be considered to be guilty of ineffective assistance of counsel if we don't ask every potential client who comes into our office; if they are a U.S. citizen or not. It is our obligation to know whether they are or they are not a U.S. citizen. If they are not a U.S. citizen, then we have an obligation, at a minimum, to tell them to also not only retain our Firm, but to also consult with an immigration lawyer as well; because the outcome of their case would cause them to lose their immigration status and be deported. So, the immigration lawyer and the criminal defense lawyer must work together.

What we want is for the immigration attorney to tell us what our non-citizen clients can, and cannot, tolerate in the final disposition of their particular type of criminal charge. We discharge our legal duty when we tell a non-citizen to see an immigration attorney immediately; but unfortunately, many non-citizens do not heed our advice and they put their chances at remaining in the U.S., or having their Green cards renewed or obtaining citizenship, in jeopardy; as they could face <u>additional</u> immigration consequences, in addition to a criminal record, jail.

As you can see, it is important that as a criminal defense attorney for any particular client, citizen or non-citizen, that potential clients must come to us in a non-defensive manner; in which they are prepared to tell us everything about the facts of their charge; their life; their jobs; what they hold dear; and what their needs are in the outcome of their case - so that we can shape our defense together as a "Team" for the very best outcome possible. We work as a Team, both with our client and ourselves as attorneys, doing our separate "Due Diligence" homework together. Therefore, combining our forces for an incredibly powerful defense on behalf of our client. The vast majority of the many thousands of cases that I and my firm have handled for nearly 30 years have resulted in an outcome that was better than the potential outcome when the client first came to us. And, in fact, many of the charges that our clients have had over the years have been dismissed, *nolle prossed*, significantly reduced or resulted in "deferred judgments" which allowed the charges to eventually be dismissed. I enjoy my job even after nearly 30 years. I feel fresh and new everyday, as does my Team at my office. We are optimistic and hopeful, but realistic about the law the facts and our clients. We work for the best and plan for the worst. This combination of all things working

together as a Team results in almost always positive outcomes for our clients.

Therefore, if you have a criminal or criminal traffic charge, please contact myself or any of the lawyers on my Team at NovaLegalGroup, P.C. We will always have an attorney talk to you, on the phone, on your first call. You will not be shoveled off to a paralegal or a secretary to talk about the details of your

case. Rather, you will talk to an attorney, on the phone for an extended period of time, in fact as long as you feel like you need and want to. And then, after our initial extended phone consultation, we will invite you in for a second detailed and in-person free consultation as a follow-up, in which we will work together to design a customized "Plan of Action" for you. In addition, we offer the ability to have an Extended Payment Plan to meet the financial needs of our clients. We will work with you within your budget and financial needs, together!

DISCLAIMER

This publication is intended to be informational only. No legal advice is being given, and no attorney-client relationship is intended to be created by reading this material. If you are facing legal issues, whether criminal or civil, seek professional legal counsel to get your questions answered.

NovaLegalGroup, P.C.

1507 King Street

Alexandria, VA 22314

(703) 548-1462

www.NovaLegalGroup.com

Made in the USA
Monee, IL
05 November 2026

67385053R00050